WayPoems

WayPoems

ALLEN GODDARD

RESOURCE *Publications* • Eugene, Oregon

WAYPOEMS

Copyright © 2021 Allen Goddard. All rights reserved. Except for brief quotations in critical publications or reviews, no part of this book may be reproduced in any manner without prior written permission from the publisher. Write: Permissions, Wipf and Stock Publishers, 199 W. 8th Ave., Suite 3, Eugene, OR 97401.

Resource Publications
An Imprint of Wipf and Stock Publishers
199 W. 8th Ave., Suite 3
Eugene, OR 97401

www.wipfandstock.com

PAPERBACK ISBN: 978-1-6667-1911-6
HARDCOVER ISBN: 978-1-6667-1912-3
EBOOK ISBN: 978-1-6667-1913-0

NOVEMBER 19, 2021

For Roger

Contents

Promptings

Evening wind | 3
Awoken | 4
Naming *ex nihilo* | 6
Consider | 8
Newness | 9
Things look up | 10
Laying out a Labyrinth | 11
Humpback on Iona Beach | 12
Creation Mourns the Lonmin Massacre | 14

Memory Work

Set like flint | 23
Elusive memory | 24
Whitfield | 25
Outside inside Charisea | 26
Record of decision | 28
Journeying towards Durban's COP 17 in the Season of Creation | 30
Extinction | 31
Prayers in pains of Polar Bears | 32
Recapitulation | 34
Into the tsunami | 36
New pathway | 38
Black Walnut | 40
Eagle mending | 41

In Answer

Cumberland kalimba | 45
Toad crossing | 46
Art in the Park | 47
Hill Sixty waits | 48
Black swan gardening | 50
Whoever has ears | 51
Quince abundance in a neglected garden | 52
Wind on the Bainskloof Witterivier | 53
Trust of heart | 54
Jonathan moment | 56
Sons and daughter | 57
O happy day! | 58
Waiting for the consolation | 60
Eye has not seen | 62
Gelassenheit | 64
Worthiness | 65
Hidden spectacle | 66
Axis Mundi, approaching Passover | 68
Eloi! Eloi! Lama sabachthani? | 69
Before death incognito, on Holy Saturday | 70
Easter visitation | 71
Pilgrim | 72

Acknowledgements | 74

To the Reader

Attentiveness to life and memory, with growing care for place, are at the heart of this collection. The poems are fragments of my story, memories, and sacred journey. My hope is that they rekindle many little counter-moments of delight or joy or lament, in our age so burnt out by indifference, displacement, ennui and despair. The more I traverse recurring griefs or walk into unexpected joys in life's mystery, I turn to prayer, like some of these poems do. So, the cost and surpassing consolation of living into God's larger story, beholden to life's prior questions, and ever more fully in place, I offer you, to share in these pages.

Promptings

Evening wind

On my haunches in headwater grass
above the Bloukrantz at dusk
   my fingers cup
from a northwester
   nine petal starlets
   pollen pricks of yellows
bursting from whites

Their fragrance
bold at the approach of night
turns a doe downwind
   nose up, scenting no danger
   only hidden topographies
of spring-new nectar

My palm releases
these filaments, flowers
to new calls of evening surrounds
   and I rise bereft
   but at my going
twilight from their galaxy
lingers

Awoken

Was it padded claws on clicking tiles?
   Or canine whispers whined
with more than dogs'
full bladders needing out?
   Or bathroom shower drips
that hinged me out of bed
   or something else?

Did Venus wedged in black
between the bedroom curtains
   or distant Perspex heartbeats
of the kitchen clock
   or ice gusts through a backdoor push
of paws, and biting feet
   arouse my new resolve to write?

Or was it moving house
that opened boxed ideas
and blew off journal dust
   to retrospect what's past?
   Did pitching junk and sudden midnight
countdowns to the future's big removal vans
awake new thoughts to ask

What life sounds waken pens?
What loves, new thresholds
   doorways, visitations
more ordinary
than sorrow slow in parting?
   Do poets simply answer fading
whispers of their names?

As Samuel barefoot
to a beckoning
   braved his three departures
into consecrating night
   so these stirrings stumble
on some summoned phrases
   written into dawning light

Naming *ex nihilo*

Since birth
until the moonless night
they burst the bank of gorse and lichen
to the bog below
their slatted Yorkshire barn
   this flaxen boy with plaintive kestrel
and warning Collie
   has uttered not a sound

His peering father branching
out on drawing quicksand
   knots the ankle of his son, and, joined
through writhing mist
   spread-eagled, panting hard
they reach the mud-smeared mane
   a white mare still alive but prone
on horror, like some future Tollund find

No voice but husks of whispers
   boy-breath on her flaring nostrils
raise two pointed, shadowed ovals
   ears once straight in daylight
   pert into the moor's curved blue
now dun and spattered
   jolt towards the deep
and sucking terror

His first word is her name in blackness
   soft, wind-carried, vowelled
more clearly than the sheepdog's yap
   the sudden raptor shriek, incredulous
   as if it all flapped up
into the coming down of angels
   his rising intone clears the ruckus
   breaks some inner, equine trap

She moves, a phantom wreck
submerged in breaking murk
and torpid, popping bubbles
   then finds unlikely ground
   She powerfully rears into the child's first
dropping shout delayed a lifetime
   altos haltered tightly round
her pitching jawline stubble

A sodden father staggers, cold
and sobbing, stiffly scuffing
stones onto the heath
   He trails the dimming rump
   the dog, the bird, and disappearing
feet and legs akimbo, and
joy, still dragging, just emerging
out of numbing disbelief

Consider

Is there a parable in eyes
that catch on eagles
   ears that turn
to sounds of doves
   or pulsing hearts in hands
that scoop and raise a fallen mannikin?
   Or, when weavers overhang
their craft on palms
or bulbuls shuffle clerodendrum baubles
   scolding winter bees still nosy
after last year's summer mauves are gone?

And what of ring-necks' clinks
on stainless steel
for dog-abandoned scraps
   or puff-backs' loud *Eurekas!*
punctuating tumbled sugar paragraphs
of sunbird gossip?
   Or that looming airless silence
   the rabid Gymnogene
that hackles grounded barks
   frenzies frantic feathers
out of tunnel branches in mahogany?

Yes! All of these
   like sparrows fledged near Galilee
   will boldly kite Earth's fabrics of
the deepest friendliness in breezes
   underneath our tamed wild
suburban
leaves

Newness

In this garden postage stamp of habitat
   a montane fringe of lawn and rockery
   three milk-and-honey summers'
patient local plantings
could not usher changes slow enough
   before we leave
   for nature's feathered fencers

And yet today
   surprise in gasps
reminds forgotten waiting
   This little flash of darting amethyst
    a sun-refracting knight
fends aloe inflorescence
with his harmless foil

Beyond what I had hoped to hear
   so soon, like crystal
in a chandelier
   the sunbird parries bulbine
   dazzles pelargonium
and delights at secret quaffs
in such quick quenching

Things look up

The tin and flagged veranda
wrapping Alexandra Road Police Station
stifles even January's
insect stopping heat
   Yet not that far, there jaunts a song
of striped canaries
   taunting mischiefs hiding
in bedraggled Jacarandas

I slow as long it takes to stop
   lift eyes and lower
haste's horizon
   pause
to nod to mind
the mellow
acumen of Solomon

These feathered upbeats have no cares
   let alone some urgent sweaty pages
for a Commissioner of Oaths

Laying out a Labyrinth

Laying out a labyrinth
takes early morning
tramped dog droppings
   cold crust caramel
between the toes
in pre-dawn frosts
   so, not just walking, waking

Discovering the pathway
needs more than wistful strolls
   those cheerful outsets to idyllic hikes
or long ends' satisfied exhaustions
   resting in unlikely times of day
   or care with maps, uneven paths
in turns to cutbacks
   or being alert for spirals, crossings
   cul-de-sacs

Reaching the centre
will take stepping stones
and making bridges
   secateurs in thorns and hedges
   patience picking pricking Blackjacks
and openness to wait, on grief, then keeping on
in welcome, wide embrace and laughter
   faring ever, never far alone
from morning-star-eyed company

Humpback on Iona Beach

Out of the
Salish Sea
she broke water
into air
   one purpose in her
last aborted breach
   she beached
to rest herself
in death
and not be
drowned

The mystery
that splays
from such an
unbecoming beast
   wet on silver flats
   is now too every-day a tragedy

Far, and far too long in not
disentangling
her thrash
at snaring trawling lines
   her freedom
snagged
   her powers all but snapped

And so, she lies, leviathan
   sun-salt raw in lacerations
   yet strangely safe
on warming
ground

Eventually
   she cuts free
from breath itself
   in a visitation more than
all the crying, curious
touches from two hundred
little hands
the earth so quickly
found

Unfettered now
   with no cry
of dereliction
   down
into Pacific deeps
she dips
   into her
final
sound

Creation Mourns the Lonmin Massacre

16 August 2012

I   Silence

Today
more than forty
brothers, fathers, sons
are gone
   in ricocheting silence
shouting, for that instant
after gunners'
horizontal hail

Our nation pauses
   looking on
   sitting, standing, mute
   as broadcast news
in nine official languages
hollowly intones
against the sacred stillness
   parliaments
of glib condolence
   and SAFM's *Money Web*
scouts market opportunities
in the drop and surge
in platinum

But wives and
daughters, mothers, sisters
mourn - a family extended
in this grip of quiet
   spent, in choking pits
and sinking stalls
between each
sudden new
paroxysm
of grief

Even fleeing
wielders of machetes
   trembling
ranks of stifled men
in helmets
   issue rifles smoking
in their quiet aftermath
of thunder, know
   that they will never get away
   from what this
long, awed
silence
says

II   Rocks

Columnists
quibble numbers
in this tragedy
　as if in wars
of conquest
waged or fled
　The official tolls
are meaningless
to rocks
the dead
were drilling
　or sand
so stained
which only hours ago
was brimming
with their
blood

Should there
somehow
have been
no witness left
with terror
to forget
　these very
rocks
at Wonderkop

would well recall
vain pledges strong men
trampled
in these
fallen faces
   and call out
in earshot of
complicit
coming
generations
   to longing
earth
   and knowing
heaven
   the dead
and living
rolls
of
names

III   Platinum

White Gold
shudders
   being crushed
and wants
to hide
its flash
on earlobes
necks or fingers
   hates having
to encase the stuff
of mass destruction
   balks at clinking
heard in loud
insomniac investors' dreams
   at outsourced
wages that demean
   loathes its lining
on these
white-hot bullets
   dreads the
swallowed
cries of orphans
   the coughed up
silicosis shreds
   when health-and-fitness
is for others
just another
corporate perk

   and shrinks
from all those ways
in acrid holes
that break a man
   yes, flinches from
the daily deaths
relived in the
descending cage
   and wishes it
were deaf
   to rising
prayers
of widows
   and blind
to all
these drill men
cradled
on the
ground
   but dead

Memory Work

Set like flint

The mountain sides
bend against a hot wind
drier than *Simouns*
that blew on Jonah

Bushes strain their holds
on clodding soil
in grasses fraying into dust
for dearth of rain

It looks as though
the very peaks prepare
for their figurative
quaking into sea

Yet they will
withstand
this beating
   sure, and cling
to heaven
earthing, waiting
for the coming feet

Elusive memory

On a steep rise, after we turn to Bathurst
in what was Grahamstown
   a lead pane window restaurant jukebox
like a gaudy wardrobe, sparkles invitation
   lit behind the ring and swing
of door-glass

Our Karoo-road chatter, hotboxed
on the Opel Record's baking seats
   enters, slows an instant, cools
as bare feet lump on red, clean vinyl
   then argues elbows onto blotched linoleum
   squeezing in to catch the back-door breeze
on soft pad-button-booths for six

We choose from blissful visions
   waffles, syrup, cream and tea, and wait
to five-cent tunes of Forty Fives, in tapping Pop
   each song reflecting crimsons, blues
   and orange neons in our faint-wide faces

Pressing cheeks fixate on slide-drop armatures
   whirling chrome, our fingers on the bass-beats
pulsing in the speakers' weave and spars of oak
   three faces all but hiding in this dance-floor
capsuled wonder of the Sixties

Still only hills away from harbour, sand
   the sound of sea and tidal pools of holidays
   the grownups stroll but we career like flashing tops
under the door's bell-jingles, glowing
   like those now receding jukebox lights

Whitfield

Trevor Lovegreen's riding school went all aflame
later afternoons when wet pans blazed in reeds
behind the gates, silos, woodchip heaps and lunging ring

Once last gymkhana dusts
had blown late leavers home
   we rode out bareback for an hour that lasted
ankle deep in solitudes of coots and grebes
   rainbows blinding splashing sun
   Our horses rocked and lunged
like unfurled schooners

You had to periscope and cling
   baptized together laughing
deep into the sodden black
and up again
   all trickling with the sunset
   churning watercress and tossing lilies
flung into the halos of the West

In the far shallows we turned, full gallop
   back, to white-eyed, whinnied sawdust
   hooves bent, bucking air, and rolling ears
alert to clanks on concrete
   buckets, stablers' clicks and
wafting scents of sorghum, peanuts, teff

Then, one last necking down of moonlit brushes
   fresh snorts in warming hay
   and a long unspoken, soft and velvet parting

Outside inside Charislea

Opening
the veranda sliding glass
   time again
unlocks the dawn's
gold bars of garden

Cold wind feathers in
this final chance
to be just here
   yet also
out there
venturing
the grass horizons

Across this threshold
lazy spring
   only just still sleeping
   cannot wake
to shed
procrastinating
Pecan
   or shake off winter
sheets of frost
   Both seasons
   but within arms' reach
are joined today, beyond
this lintel wind chime breeze
in thawing sun

In still short coming days
we leave
    These pollard frames
on veld-scenes will recede
    obscured
inside
remembering

Yet this day-brink somehow
will remain disclosing
    never further out
than just this single step ahead
and beckoning
    to linger in
and contemplate
a cup of morning
coffee

Record of decision

Since young Victoria
   polo fields have turfed
the Pietermaritzburg Dorpspruit
floodplain, like an ancient oval
of the Commonwealth

However, just the other day
our city planners' north-south
'corridor of development'
redefined this plover's park
   as 'prime'

The polo set ran discontent
while interested, affected parties
baited city sentiment
   Surprisingly, the Council motioned
players, horses
and Jacaranda commons
should remain, 'as heritage'

Yet, not long after
   before the dawn one day
   some tractor tracks
cut deep into a century
in sediment

So now, in place of weekly morning markets, meets
    and almost all the birds but egrets
    instead of horses, bales, marquees and hot-ice boxes
rubble creeps in mounds with Blackjacks
    oil-cans, *Khakibos* and rotting refuse

And masking these are concrete, tin
and gleaming sales floors
    redbrick condescending onto lawns
and pampered beds
    all locally indigenous
but not reflecting well
in sepia glass
    on neon billboard alleys
flashing lookalikes
of urban facelifts
yet to come

Our city yeomen of the now
have ploughed and scattered
once-a-life-time flood lines
    with their faceless futures, pensions
    venture finance, sprawling
hastily but not sustainably
as what remains
    what weeds remember
of the fields

Journeying towards Durban's COP 17 in the Season of Creation

For two thousand years our story said
there was no room at the inn
   but what if there were none
within the stable
for the aardvark,
   or the cud and rumble
of a pachyderm,
   or in the manger
for the velvet shrew
   or on the sawdust
for a plaintive nightjar pair?

Would skies be clean enough
to find a guiding star?
Would Earth still reap
forgiving hay for comfort
or well clean water for a birth?

Extinction

The little boy in greeting doesn't hide
such curiosity concealed
behind his *isiZulu* answer

With just two syllables
of his mother's tongue
   he looks down - reduced

But now, and standing tall
he tells me straight in mine
   his second one

My smile's the prize that he has won
   but some hidden grain that only germinates
in soils of idiom, is gone

Prayers in pains of Polar Bears

Christ
   companion of the wild
near me, on winter veld
   while somewhere summer's she-bear
pants at thinning cracks
   her will and weight collapse
for fear of drowning strength
   to swim
her way's return

Jesus
   of foxes, snakes, of doves
   who knows the bear's mute pain
   her breathless groans that hate deceit
in futile winds from warming south
   her weak, light-headed loss
of paths primordial as ice
   Her listless swaying
weighs my breath

Weeping servant
of the burdened cross
   your crown's unfinished passion, your grief's
long torment for my injury and thorns
   your sore and streaming side
where blood and water
flowed to soil
   these seed
my wrenching, dying

Stricken
   left, you drank of hyssop wine
for lifting seas' acidic dross
   Your parched slaking
pricks my thirst
   Your last echo chastens
   stops my tongue

God's only son
   cut loose from Spirit
   then dropped asphyxiating
to Sheol
   breathe on us who tread
the frozen precipice
   who flail at hope near the abyss

Unlikely gardener of God
   bend toward Earth's living dust
   and see, take in our lost approach
before the falling down of stars
   before your final call
to wade eternal wetlands
   Herald of our world's exchange
   emancipate
all breath from pacing gloom
   unscale distracted eyes to unseen roads
   our homestretch smiling in your brow

Recapitulation

Has anyone seen the garage-door-keys?
   Dad, they're always in your pockets, jacket, desk or
      briefcase
   Sweetheart, have you left them on your shaving shelf?
Oh thanks, but actually they're not!

Dad, I saw them with your library cards and glasses
   Have they fallen in the garden at your ladder by the
      hedge
or by your mileage book inside the car or cubby hole?

Sweetie, are they wedged or propped
 or put forgotten, dropped
   down by the ironing board
    or maybe
     in
    your denims
   at the bottom of the
 bathroom laundry pile or in the
window – or have you tried the kitchen sink?

Come off it guys! They wouldn't fit straight down the plughole!
Ag no! And where's the new Q20 can? Has someone seen the
   new Q20 spray to lubricate the garage lock again?
It looks as though it will not budge!

Oh, just have a look! Aren't they always where they usually
   are?
The Q20 can is on the cleaning shelf!

Your keys are sometimes hanging on the kitchen calendar
or in the key pile in the key bowl!

Ja ... okay ... but actually they're not.

Has someone seen the rare and gentle, charismatic Cape Parrot, Oribi, the Blue Swallow or the satin of a Karkloof Blue?
They aren't where they usually are, in montane highlands Ngongoni grass or forest; nowhere in the mist belt zones!

    But aren't they always high
      over
       there, where
     many
    other
   creatures
recognize their greens
   and topaz
    lovely
     opals
      just like
       rescue
        ships that hoist their little flags when sailing by?

... Oh no! Where will ever there be found
a true, beyond-the-call-of-duty smith
to work the locks imprisoning the Earth?
Where on Earth you say? That's actually what I've been asking ...
But ... wait! ...   ... *There it is or rather*
   ... there ...   ... *he is ... ...*
stretching out! ...   ... *There! ...*
But can it really be? ...
... He's dying!

Into the tsunami

Why even pretend at fearless
when this wave, fast-rising
panics
billions
fleeing fear itself
afraid?

Stop
all directives for control
Accept dependence
Breathe
no word towards the looming gulf
the mounting crest

Release
sighs' empathies
with Earth's neuralgic diaphragm
Stand
against the tragedy
of loves beleaguered

Taste
of tears
not throat-hard anger
Touch
like tender eyes
will wake a child

Give way
into the
first great crash towards oblivion
Dare
cling to weakness sinking
flooding holds to trust

Freefall
into life's departing
breath
then hear and answer
Jesus
praying for the world

New pathway

Migrant worker millions traverse India and Bangladesh
   halfway home in starved invisibility and they are blocked
   Palestine is packing, sending masks to Israel
and getting bullets, bulldozed olive groves and settlers
armed with pumps of human waste, as thanks

Bergamo, London, Tehran, Cape Town, Delhi and New York
   the world avoids the hidden wings of death
Turkey, Saudi and the Gulf maintain a telling silence
   China wakes to world recession
and Zimbabwe totters once again, but now from on its knees
   Gazans, Uyghurs, Yanomami and Rohingya
   all Earth's prisoners and warders
fly in dreams, hoping to free themselves awake
and only speak of nightmares

Where are the paths through wilderness?
The streams in desert?

A Santiago Puma fleets in city glass against the Andes' snow
    Captive Beijing pandas' first-time mating is in solitude
    Dolphins play with sighs from tied up gondolas
unmanned, on Venice waterways
    Shy deer nudge at curiosities in Boston parks
and wild boar snuffle hopes of truffle,
on Barcelona boulevards

Duiker middens sprinkle steam on Durban's tree-lined curbs
while Penguins - new pedestrians - dawdle into Simonstown
    Low smog lifts Los Angeles and Nepali Himalayas
like years of dust from long forgotten bridal veils
    An eagle scatters doves in Sydney's urban penny gums
while starlings rafter silence without traffic noise
    high inside Makhanda's empty Holy Week Cathedral

Nguni cattle on the High Street low
    so where will Earth's such long awaited
holy ones now go?

Black Walnut

Why bare-arms
   the only arboreal thing
with not a bud
to share in verdanting
this garden's forest spring?
    But reaching, still, and long past dried-up winter
    why stark, and even after rain?

This tree has stature, girth
and prime position
   yet seems in mourning, leafless, waiting

There is some hidden purpose
slow to wet its drought
in deepest rings
   to waken sap
   burst green and shout
a shooting grandeur

Dark and naked now
   it points so strangely small
and stolid
through its window
to the clouds, still not
reviving last year's
greenest memory

Eagle mending

Set free to early morning
from a holding box
   caged weeks in recovery
   a young black eagle
blunders into brightness

Slow fulfilling wings
splay and lift her
groping to an anthill
   but she topples
clowning on low grasses

Dark pinions bright again
   this time to winds
that gift her eager reach
and launch her eyes
to search translucent canopies

So, she thermals easily
   to tame again her wilderness
of burnished blue

In Answer

Cumberland Kalimba

At an updraft where canyon boulders
pediment a ledge of cliff-burnt
rock-fig leaves
   in sprawls of honeysuckle
high, thick berry trusses rustle
   Trumpeter Hornbills
necking, feisty, feeding

My wind-borne thrums of altos
flush out loud, bird-baby cries
and animate some butterflies
like tumbling flashes of some Eucalyptus leaves
   black zig-zagging white and blue
in dappled light
on airing silence underneath

As wailing birds scold gravity
   the hornbill fleet now dips and crests away
a wake of wind that warms my face
   and lifts my thumb-notes
only one prayer's reach
out from the sill beneath my feet
   up into high billows, on bending grace

Toad crossing

Strolling a Hilton track
   twilight
almost spent
   I glimpsed the landing shadow
of the year's first toad
heading off
from reed frog's
pipes, and bullfrogs' crow-songs
flirting on the wind

Did you
feel a flash of silver
rumble in your belly
   some far valley thunder
   then hurdle disappointed
little patch leopard
past my feet?

You squatted
long enough
to get my greeting
gentle
off my haunches
   then sprang into
the hiding dusk
   so quick
as if
unimpressed
by the chorus on the lake
   all mettle out of sync
   and wrong
about the rain!

Art in the Park

Nearly a decade since we first scuffed leaves
along this African Montmartre
    why straggle on again with last day-trippers
visiting the Msunduzi's
River Seine?

Now you pay an entrance fee
to see the city's
"multi-digit-turnover attraction"
    and even so, a dogging sense of déjà vu
defrauds us, slowly

Carnivals of oils and panorama aquarelles
    but where's a misfit like Gauguin
and why no luckless local
lunar-struck van Gogh?
    Only well-fed, wined and sleepy pedlars

Like wind-wrapped Magi, weary
    lately recognise a cul-de-sac
    we leave at sunset in the gloaming starlight
    searching still and
certain, hoping for an icon

Hill Sixty waits

Hill Sixty waits
after sundown's
vaulting Amatola shadow
for one last dusk robin
and a walker calling into wind
with her leash
to be gone

Hill Sixty waits
while Leo leaps
Makhanda's furthest koppies
and wary duiker breath
dews moon-lamped dandelion
for a lapwing's
last morse cry

Hill Sixty waits
just before the dawn
for the brush of porcupines
sweeping prints from paths
their night has taken
at the waking
of a town

Hill Sixty waits
all spring, for golden
daisies lighting Pig's Ear
under webs that glisten
heather hiding
freesia
to be found

Hill Sixty waits
long since the feel
of rhino, wildebeest and lion
for aged guardians
of quarry and old kiln stacks
to legislate green
heritage

Hill sixty waits
in grass that bends northwest
and smells Antarctica
for long expected footfalls
ringing in unending rest
that harvests
holiness

Black swan gardening

Wild asters' mild roots
pull so easily through veld path dew
   yet my stoop feels like a theft
these dead pan days
   waiting on their stalks to graft
and root into my garden's
plethora of destinies

My alibi stories heroic rescues
   thrill-bent bikers' churning trails
with no clue, flattened herbs, orchids
   night-time boot piles
   mowed grass, ivy, cannas, Kikuyu
and always the detritus of lazy builders
suffocating harebells

What's more, I tell myself
   wildflowers never just escape
like all their myriad living satellites
   fleeing from our urban
footprint's diminishing returns

And my misgivings
   breathed like confessions on these twigs
into steaming grass, now find a pardon
   slim shimmers of the daybreak
halo emerald round the first new leaf

Whoever has ears

So easy
it is
living here
between affluence and hunger
green valleys of promise, fullness
and corrugated, rutted dearth
like soil-cracked fingers fumble coins
for the smallest bag of sugar -
only if we lift our eyes
to distant hills, indifferent
deaf to the summons
from the highest fathom
of the skies
whose cipher answers
the
wretched
of the
earth

Quince Abundance in a Neglected Garden

Sun swells from off the Little Karoo
in ruddy bent-borne fruit
   only just above the ground
this long, last trimester
of Cape diurnal heat

Dawn, splayed through gate rust
   dapples every pear-like apple
   leafing homey scents
all bunched in secret
riping goodness

Today, an onshore wind
will launch the cloddy asteroids
into pungent atmospheres
   orbit trails
   leaf-litter clouds

While yesterday's
   wheel in universes
yet unventured
   except a battered padlock frees
my new trajectory into their shades

My bent approach
jerks and slows in clicking knees
   searches shadows' hints of faces
   then, haunches steady, laughs alight with
new acquaintance

Wind on the Bainskloof Witterivier

A ruffling Southeaster
soon after dawn
ripples a Wellington mountain pool
   to wake and blink white
as if light sprayed on such deeps
   gusts on God's presence
dazzling, into a question

Unfreighted rocks afloat
under the pool face
   lift every heaviness out of my gaze
   so that I can answer
the frankness
   the bluster
of this river's youth

And what do I say?

Yes!
   I am here to be
torrent roughed, tousled and cooled
like today's first sun sprinkled
   heeding God's voice over water
like a lad, half-clad, whoops
ankle deep in the daybreak
and then, finding breath
   leaps

Trust of Heart

A sultry afternoon, July
and after lunch - olive savours
   fetta, rocket, fish cakes
   hidden bougainvillea wine
in the Algarve's Ferragudo

An invite to walk
with some sense
of peregrination - this hot day
   finding our way with no cell phones
to Praia dos Caneiros

We set out fresh companions
of rolling scrub, primrose, gravel
   towards modest cliffs
   the sea's vast mirror
warming welcome
   no dark forbidding
like at Moher

Our down-path to umbrellas
   sun folk, ice creams
between cheap cameras
   is seamless, to shingles
licked by the surf

New joy plashes
   unfolds our immersion
in lazy breast strokes far out
to ochre stacks
splashed into sky

Bobbing becalmed, in sea swelled luxury
   delicious, anonymous
   treading further yet, out from home
   and footloose, only on such
Mediterranean safety

Waves pull to the sandstone
   haul us breathless
   dripping contentment
for this rock, a rest
and our new colloquium
of sea rush, unoiled wailings of gulls
   shy gestures
   playful questions
in first bonds, a forming of friends

We taste scores of silences
   salted, satisfied
   unscheduled
and utterly whole
until day's dipping bronzes our limbs

Finally, our dive into silver, the plunge
   for as long and as deep as we may
   under the coming close of day
   in one gold, strong, slow surfacing
to our return

Jonathan moment

When I
name a taste
from the brown well
I sometimes
pause at
in your eyes
   I am shy
to look
too deep

To dip once more
and slowly
drink

In the clear
reflection
   your
smiling gift
inviting
me to be refreshed
   is also
mine
to give

Sons and daughter

The little girl I never fathered
gazes from her own reflection
   eager, up
to the waterline
bending hazel eyes
   Her freckled
nose is rippling

Candace, Hannah, Cherith
   playfully I have named her
when locked incompletion
opens quite unexpected
feather breaths
   or hop, skip and shy scents
somehow squeal
quick-phrased delights of her

Her young shape matures
to a woman's curious poise
in a moment, a ripple of reverie
   and her whisper
drops onto
her watery self
   slowly rising

And what is your Father's name?

O happy day!

The day
to walk away
from every seminar
or nary hour on *Leadership*
arrives
after a relinquished
sun
in daylight's leaving
   not easy, nice
   but waits out
pain that's
easing
past
   is whole at dusk
in choosing
tears
   and turns
in dark
   to letting go
all pent-up words
   releasing even
being prepared to leave
what's hardest
   not forgetting

When twilight's
final incandescence
dies
under the milky spill
of earth-new
night
   I tread
this un-mooned
hemisphere
   and only
a memory's seed
   of
trust
   to the morning
   I
drop
faithfully
to ground

Waiting for the Consolation

Old Simeon
and Anna deaf
   sit in resounding quiet
at some Herodian arch
or Temple colonnade
   surrounded by echelons
of highly turbaned men
who court theology careers
with watchful eyes
on market
shares

Diminutive giants
at prayer
   so out of place
in all this trading
   they bow unnoticed
   washed in shrouds
of skylight beams
   hidden in their shadows'
stillness

They have gone about
the longings of their lives
anonymous, content
   pressing on and bent
towards that once
and future hindsight
   that points ahead

like an inkling of the joy of slipping past
yet recognizing that one thing
we all are born for
   and knowing in the grief
   when it has passed
that we arrived
   that finally
we are
darkening
a bright threshold
of the inner courts
of One
   whose new grace nears us
   lets us go
that step across
   in peace

Eye has not seen

Her daily death is endless blood
on underclothes she's lumbered
   stooped, three-decade-listless
limbs recalling
   borne, defending hidden body blows

Unkempt as carrying lice is shamed
outside the gates
   she eats with freaks
   hermaphrodites
and lepers

Yet not so burdened
as to scuffle garbage
   darken alleys
one last downcast
tattered drag of sacking
   out of cobbled shadows
to a public square

She braves the gasps
   the glare of stench in sun
   dares one more repelling
to collapse and reach
the Rabbi

What this little town
has always known, rejects
   and needs no proof of, now unravels
in the thread of weave
   his seamless cloak

In just one word
that boldens blood
and lifts her from his feet
   he shuts, forever
opens, like love's delight
at last in life-long waiting eyes

And thus he snuffs
the gaudy folkish tinder box
of tongues

Daughter . . .

Gelassenheit

All that
principled ink
spilled on *Christian Calling*
in no end of books
can stop flowing dry

And rather read
a clamber
into tales of sweaty camel hide
   frying locusts, honey
in the wilderness
   towards the voice on Jordan, sounding strong
then silenced by a prison's breath

On, to the hiss of braising fish and stick-bread
   shoreline gusts of baritones
and waves' slow runnelling at stones
   discarded boats in shallows
   To sandy squeaks of footprints
   fragrant ashes, Turkish coffee
   and all those basket loads of breakfast

To getaways in dousing coals
   forsaking paths
yet close on heels
on ways however unforeseen
   whoever hunts, whatever stalks
the outlaws
   and their Nazarene

Worthiness

Even John the Baptizer
overthought, fretted
   questioned double-doubts
with time enough to hear blind confines
   smell his chains of doom
and feel new trust in age-old hope
ache at the forsaking

His messengers' voices
spiral down into his vault, his damp despair
   sibilants of snippet phrases
   flares of news like starlit wonders, healings
   goodness showering untouchables
   enthralling ragged crowds
in feasting surges

Then comes a clear, familiar cadence
   the Rabbi epigram directed
   dropped like mocking pebbles plumb
a cistern's echoes – much too long
for one on pain of death
and cracking hard and loud
to bottom on this hole's forgotten
   words to kindle dry desire
but cold on steeled resolve

A last hard saying, wet in wilderness
   My deaf and dumb divine offense
   unravels resurrection

Hidden spectacle

Over the rise at Bethany
a donkey, her colt, suddenly halt
blinking at dropped horizons
   clean valleys new under morning

Far below, the Eastern gate
   piles of terraces, roof lines
dwarfed by gold on grandeur
   terracotta, limestone - Herod's folly
all in walls and stairs and buttresses

And pilgrims browned
   numberless as Judean sands
   not pressing off
to buy libations - doves or lambs
   but knotted, like ants in intrigues
   their sound on rising air
a cacophony of arguments

Women, children pour out to the Kidron
hoisting palms, black kilims, purple
   their *Hosannahs* hurry hundreds
crowding uphill shouts and pointings

High up the way a rider sobs
   his caravan's uneasy outline, odd
   two asses' fluffed out ears
flexed sideways
   jostle at his drab companions

Now sharpest day-heat
spears twin portcullis shadows
   blurs the coming train, sung blessings
   hazes clamour
cloaks and branches
   swallowing the dust and din and celebration

Tranquil in the human roil and sweat
of Jerusalem's golden entrance
   a deep, forgiving shade
conceals the Galilean, his unstaunched tears
   and silences an instant
   all of this crowd in loud misunderstanding
   of mourning

Axis Mundi, approaching Passover

Near early April, when Christ sets his face for Jerusalem
   both hemispheres all but equally
leave equinox
   sunrise and sunset
almost a synchrony
   the moon, near full, one night before
lamb-blood daubs lintels
gateways, thresholds
   each left deserted by
what yet could make for peace

Entering Gethsemane
   he draws back
to shadows there
   from winged darkness
   boding its appointed time

And Earth, its binary realms
and yearning borealis
   burdened seas and torn savannas
   turns by the blood
of his intercession

Eloi! Eloi! Lama sabachthani?

The final cry
sounded like
a dying Jew's
Elijah-in-delirium,
   a last-ditch clutch
at breath

But his gasp
   outcried and sharp
   was his final protest
   one last grief-wound rattled
at the lasting, searing outspan
of his comrade, Simon

It was lament
at absence
   indifference
   a holding to account
for thorns and nails
   the near approach of spears
and to the last, the splinters

It was an earthquake
warning shock
   proclaiming
to the shrouded stars
and uncloaked women
   love's unfinished
argument

Before death incognito, on Holy Saturday

Stopping on an errand
at high paddocks over
Queen Elizabeth Park
   two chestnuts
   wind-blown, grazing
   get me to brake
get out, and breathe
their views to
washed horizons

As horses do
   these proffer slow encounter
in clicks of tongue
   and prying muzzles
into hands, soft cups
and hairs on lips in licks
on fingers

But what if COVID covert, somehow near is *here!*
on Town Hill's blue-green height from city air?

O God of all Protection
let any close contagion now be nuzzled down, away
in what remains today - this standstill in between
your suffocating death and our world without end
   your grass and grace
and their free
far-roaming foraging

Easter visitation

All breath in Nineveh stood to a standstill
for a fleeting, sullen
worm of a man
   Jonah skulking accusations
from the desert scrub, mirage and haze

The African flotilla of Queen of Sheba's
train of gold and spices
answered
the renown of Solomon
   coy veils and nodding copper beads, amazed

That prophet's mocked good riddance
and all the camel fanfare for
her Sabaean majesty
   still tingle ears' astonishment
in yearning hearers weighing up their days

Yet one of greater fame than David's noble son
approaches just in passing
   arrives as if for elsewhere
   Seemingly he gently presses on
evading the distracted gaze

Pilgrim

Prompted by memories of Trevor Gow

Where farm tracks
end
at barbed wire and bushwillow
I ponder
walk
and recollect your
courage, dropped
near the
weir

So, did you
drive
the dust road and memories
of friends, or
balk
and risk one
last tar stone
tunnel
fear?

Such meagre
hope
you coined to get up here
in one piece
brave
enough
to life-let
your witheld
wanted
leave

And did your
grain
break all the sickles
dying green
where
they found
your sleeping
cradled
head?

The road you
came
is mystery, yet we
your gleaning
burdens
share
and walk on
living
dead

Acknowledgements

The poet is grateful for permission to publish here, the following poems, which were previously published in 2014 in an earlier draft, by A Rocha South Africa, in *Creation's Yes! An Anthology of Poems on Creation,* edited by Heather Johnston: "Toad Crossing," "Evening Wind," "Set Like Flint," "Record of Decision," "Creation Mourns the Lonmin Massacre," "Humpback on Iona Beach," "Wind on the Bainskloof Witterivier," "Extinction," and "Eagle Mending."

Thank you to Liz Gow for kind permission to publish the poem in memory of Trevor Gow.

Inexpressible thanks also, to soul friends who have walked alongside with open minds, listening hearts and generous dreams for my journey.

www.ingramcontent.com/pod-product-compliance
Lightning Source LLC
Chambersburg PA
CBHW071736040426
42446CB00012B/2377